How to Be a
Catholic Mother

How to Be a Catholic Mother

Bill Dodds

Illustrated by
Mark Engblom

Meadowbrook Press
Distributed by Simon & Schuster
New York

Library of Congress Cataloging-in-Publication Data

Dodds, Bill
    How to be a Catholic mother/Bill Dodds; illustrated
by Mark Engblom.
    p. cm.
    Includes bibliographical references.
    1. Mothers—Religious life. 2. Mothers—Humor.
3. Women, Catholic—Humor. I. title.
BX2353.D56   1990   282'.085'2—dc20   89-28917

ISBN: 0-88166-130-9

Editor: Bruce Lansky
Production Editor: Sandy McCullough
Art Director: Sallie Baker
Production Manager: Pam Scheunemann
Illustrator: Mark Engblom
Cover Illustrator: Bob Flaten
Simon & Schuster Ordering #: 0-671-69610-6

Published by Meadowbrook Press, 18318 Minnetonka
Boulevard, Deephaven, MN 55391.

BOOK TRADE DISTRIBUTION by Simon & Schuster, a
division of Simon and Schuster, Inc., 1230 Avenue of the
Americas, New York, NY 10020.

90 91 92 93 5 4 3 2 1

Printed in the United States of America.

For Monica Faudree Dodds, Margaret Farrell Dodds, and Terry Gallagher Faudree, three Catholic mothers who continue to show me there really is something to all this religion business.

Contents

Introduction

Welcome Back, Mom

Time flies, huh, Mom? Not that long ago your mother was trying to foist the Catholic church on you. But you were just a little too slick, a little too sophisticated, a little too smart to fall for it.

And then—God works in mysterious ways and has a twisted sense of humor—you got married and had a family and, my oh my, that started a whole new ball game.

Suddenly you needed someone to back your boot-camp approach to motherhood. You seemed to recall something from your past....

So you went searching for the church of old, but something was wrong.

Kind of like "Password." Remember? You turned on the tube, expecting to see old Allen Ludden in his horn-rim glasses, and there was that guy—you know, what's-his-name—giving you a great big grin with teeth only slightly smaller than the keys on a piano.

Proof positive that nothing is sacred.

How to Be a Catholic Mother was written for you. It's your guide to Catholicism after *Vatican Council II: The Sequel.*

Just when you thought it was safe to go back to the church.

Chapter One

Even when you ran with that wild street gang, you wore your plaid jumper and soap-and-water saddle shoes.

O Sacrament Most Holy

Baptism is that sacrament in which a couple—you and your husband—take a long, hard look at their newborn and say, "Holy Christ, now what do we do?"

This is a prayer.

God knows these words come straight from your heart.

So does terror.

This is a "graced" moment.

You hold that sweet, innocent baby and know that in no time at all she will want to wear three-inch spiked heels and move in with a biker named Psycho.

You wanted to, didn't you?

And what stopped you?

You were a Catholic. You were polite and educated and kind and happy and *followed the rules.*

Even when you ran with that wild street gang, you wore your plaid jumper and soap-and-water saddle shoes. You could never lose your Catholic roots. If someone sneezed, you were always the first to say, "God bless you."

That's what you want for your child.

What About the Guilt?

"Wait a minute," voices may be saying to you. Could it be that you did the right thing because the church laid a heavy guilt trip on you, not because you really wanted to?

Who cares? you answer.

Motherhood gives you a whole new perspective, doesn't it?

Call the Parish

Now that you've decided to do it, how do you get your child baptized?

What did your mom do?

She put on a frumpy dress, a dorky hat, and white gloves, got the clan to meet one Sunday afternoon at the back of the church, and then invited them back to the house for cake and coffee.

You can handle that.

Ask your mom to bring the cake.

And don't forget to call the local parish. How long has it been since you and your husband went to church, anyway?

Oh, my.

2

Baptism 101

You make the call and the next thing you know you're at a class on baptism taught by the pastor. But something is up. You're sure of it.

You were expecting somebody like old Monsignor Quinn, the head of your childhood parish. You'll never forget that grizzled old duke who had his smile shot off while serving as a Marine Corps sergeant in World War II.

Old Monsignor Quinn (all of 38) was six years younger than the pastor at this parish, Father Bob.

Father *Bob*?

Right now he's saying what a tough job it is being a parent today and how glad he is to see so many couples who want their children baptized. And he's mentioning how even a short visit with his young nieces and nephews really makes him appreciate celibacy.

Really "embrace" it, is how he puts it.

He laughs and says "welcome back" to those—is he looking at you?—who have been on a little sabbatical from the church.

At this point, feel free to worry.

What is this guy up to?

Pop Quiz

This is a good time for a test. Raise your hand and very innocently ask, "Father, what about going to limbo?"

Limbo, as you well know, is the name of heaven's back porch, the place reserved for all unbaptized children who die.

And he says, "Hey, mon, de parish dance be set for Saturday night. And den we all going to limbo!"

And you mutter to yourself, "Hell, I thought this was a Catholic parish!"

It's time to find out what has happened.

A New Rule Book

Once again you discover that the culprit is *Vatican Council II: The Sequel.*

Just when you thought it was safe to go back to the church.

Now you *want* rules and structures and *discipline* to help you raise your child, but they've been replaced by... by... by...

By golly, as if that's not bad enough, you have to read some books and watch a film strip and you feel as stupid as a convert.

And to top it off, Father "Bob," who looks a lot like a Smurf in a Roman collar, laughs more often than Ed McMahon.

It just ain't *natural!*

Ah, well. Go to the other class sessions and have your child baptized.

It's free.

What's in a Name?

All this "new church" stuff is well and good, but some things haven't changed. For instance, you still have to come up with a good Catholic name for your kid. That means a saint's name or one from the Bible.

"Judas" is a poor choice.

So are "Pontius Pilate" and "Herod."

"Little Caesar" is kind of cute. Especially if you want your child to open a pizza chain when he grows up.

You should *not* give your child any far-out names like the ones from the '60s. You know, "Starshine" or "One World" or "Ozone" or "Tofu."

Why not?

Because there are no Catholic saints by those names.

Solid Catholic Names

If your child is a boy, you have to name him Joseph, Michael, or John.

If she's a girl, you must call her Mary, Mary, or Mary.

Can Fido Join the Faith?

If you have older children, they may want to know if it's all right to have the dog baptized. The answer is no.

Of course they'll hold a service on their own when you're not around. Just like you did with your baby before her baptism.

It's all right. All Catholic mothers take out this form of "term insurance" in case the "whole life" policy is delayed for any reason.

You don't need to mention this to the pastor, nor should you ask him about getting a family pet baptized.

He will, however, bless your husband's putter.

The Family Baptismal Gown

It could be that you married into a family in which a baptismal gown has been handed down from generation to generation. You are expected to dress your child in this for the ceremony.

And, most likely, you've lost it.

It's not your fault. You've been a little busy lately what with another person growing inside you and then wanting to come out and all. Anyone would understand.

Except your in-laws, of course.

Here's what you do. Poke a hole in an old white pillowcase and sew on a few ruffles.

So far the only people who have ever looked closely at the gown have been each child's mother, and mothers of newborns are so whacked out they don't remember things like that. Just watch your mother-in-law cluck over the bogus heirloom, telling all kinds of lies about how her husband's grandmother brought it over from the old country.

Right.

Actually, you've done her a favor. If the pillowcase she gave you was still around, someone might look closely at it at this baptism and see the J.C. Penney label she forgot to rip out.

The label on yours says "K Mart."

Don't forget to rip it out!

Sorry About That

The next sacrament your child is up for, many years after baptism, is Reconciliation.

Is *what*?

Penance.

H*uh*?

Confession.

O*h*.

Ah, yes. The black box. Ninety-five percent of Catholic horror stories involve stepping into the confessional. You can hardly wait to push your misbehaving child that way.

Bad news. Now the sacrament of Reconciliation (confession) is celebrated face-to-face with the person and the priest just sitting there.

If the person doesn't want to literally face the music, he can choose to kneel behind a screen.

And priests hardly ever scream "*You did what!*" anymore.

Bummer, huh?

And you've been looking forward to this for years! Hell's bells, you've been keeping a list of your child's sins since he was 18 months old.

But that's not the worst of it.

Your child will probably *like* going to confession. Really. He likes going to the dentist, doesn't he? Sugar-free junk food, fluoride in the water, and toothpaste that beats the hell out of tartar keep his mouth free of cavities so he doesn't *have* to fear the dentist.

Worse yet, your child may have the same question about confession that he has about the dentist: "When are you going, Mommy?"

Oh, dear.

You say, "Mommy just went."

And add that lie to your list.

First Holy Communion

For First Holy Communion, white is in. You must dress up your seven-year-old daughter like a little bride or your seven-year-old son like a miniature milkman.

But Communion is more than a fashion event. As a Catholic mom, it's your job to know some of the history of it. In the early part of this century, Pope Pius X said it was okay for little kids to receive Communion. Before that, for a long time, children didn't receive the host for the first time until they were teenagers.

(Of course, this was years ago when teenagers actually went to Mass. If you find that shocking, consider this: So did husbands. It goes without saying that this was before televised sports.)

Anyway, after Pope Pius X, little kids could receive Communion. But they, like everybody else, were not allowed to eat or drink anything from midnight until after Mass.

That's why little children used to faint regularly at Sunday Mass and why your grandma sent you that First Communion card with a note that said, "God bless you, dear. I hope you didn't bump your head when you hit the floor."

In *your* day it was a three-hour fast.

Now it's only an hour.

Why do you need to know all this? Because your child will want to eat a bowl of Rice Chex 45 minutes before Mass begins, fig-uring that Communion time—half an hour into Mass—is still an hour and 15 minutes away.

The little pharisee.

If you carefully explain the history and teaching of the church regarding fasting and receiving Communion, you can kill a good 20 minutes and then say, "Well, it doesn't matter anyway. It's too late now."

Yeah, But...

Right about that time, your husband will inhale an English muffin, and then go to Communion.

How do you explain this to your child?

You say: "It doesn't matter because Daddy is going to hell anyway."

Of course.

Your kid suspected that all along.

Confirmation

In your day, kids in the seventh grade were confirmed. Nowadays teens are confirmed. And there has been another change. The candidates are no longer lightly slapped on the cheek by the bishop as part of the ceremony.

But remember, it's good for young Catholics to know the history of their church. You might want to give your teen a taste of that old-time religion.

Matrimony

What? You're already thinking about your child growing up and getting married, about having the house to yourself? Jumping the gun a bit, aren't you?

Go change your baby's diaper.

Holy Orders

This means priesthood. At times there seems to be confusion over whether the "orders" refer to giving them or taking them.

In any case, it's always a good idea to have a priest in the family. Encourage any child leaning in this direction.

Well, not "any."

Your daughter might have a tough time.

Last Rites

The "last rites" aren't the "last rites" or "Extreme Unction" anymore. Now it is the "Anointing of the Sick" or the "Sacrament of the Sick."

In the good old days, a poor, dying soul would hang on and on and on until his family thought he would never croak so they would call the priest. The sick person would see the good padre come walking through the bedroom door and die of fright.

Today the "last rites" are more like the "I-don't-feel-so-hot rites." Don't be concerned if one of your children suggests you consider receiving this sacrament.

Just try to get a little more rest.

And, as long as he's so interested in the sacraments, show him what the bishop used to do at confirmation.

Chapter Two

What the "ushers" are doing during the sermon.

Mass Confusion

Some people in your household might not want to attend Sunday Mass. Look for little signs that betray their hesitance, like somebody hysterically screaming, "I *hate going to church!* I *won't go!* You *can't make me!*"

After your husband has stopped yelling, and before your children begin, carefully explain to your kids why they must go to Mass.

It's not because God created the universe in six days and rested on the seventh. It's not because Moses came down from a mountain with ten commandments, one of which said, "Keep holy the Lord's Day."

The reason is "Because I said so."

On the Way to Church

Your children always fight during the drive to church, don't they? What kind of a mother are you! That sure doesn't happen in anybody else's family! When other cars pull into the parking lot, you don't hear those moms saying, "All right, that's it, I've had it, just stop it, stop it, *stop it!* We're going to Mass now and you're going to be good or I'll *kill you!*"

You bet your life you never heard that coming from other cars. Those moms know enough to keep the car windows rolled up.

Good Morning, Father

Always remember that your husband and children don't care if they get to Mass on time. "It's a rerun," they'll remind you. Remember, too, that the good pastor, standing guard at the back door, won't raise his eyebrows and gently tap his wristwatch at them.

Getting them there on time is *your* job, his face will tell you. Just as it was his mom's. And if she hadn't called the rectory first thing this Sunday morning, he'd still be in the sack.

As a matter of fact, she had to call twice.

Suppose There's a Miracle

If you ever do get them there on time, you'll be assured a happy, though early, death. With a smile and an "I don't believe it," you'll keel over from the shock.

Of course, you can be sure they'll be late for your funeral.

Don't Be Frightened

Maybe your children are still pretty young and all this seems upsetting to you. In that case, enjoy going to Mass with your little ones and having them scream like banshees through the whole service.

Notice how they are particularly offensive during the Father's homily on family life, when he's explaining how Hitler probably would have been an accountant if it hadn't been for his mother.

You have two options here:

1. Act deaf.

2. Take your tyke to the "crying room." This is a glassed-in room in the back of the church where children share germs and moms just like you gather to lament their lost youth and hopeless lives.

A Few Basics

Here are a few items on Sunday Mass culled from "Ask St. Monica," a very popular column in the Catholic press. As you and all good Catholic mothers know, Monica was St. Augustine's mom. Augustine was a real no-good noodnik, and Monica kept on his case for 17 years.

She wore him down, and now they are both saints.

Dear St. Monica,

I keep trying to get my family to Mass on time, but always at least one of my children can't find a shoe just when it's time to leave. What would you do?

Harried

Dear Harried,

Little Gus used to try that one on me. I finally started keeping a bedroom slipper near the front door. I would tell him to put it on and limp into church. One time he whined, "But I don't have to limp." I fixed that.

Monica

Dear St. Monica,

My children sometimes misbehave during Mass. I whisper chilling threats to them, but they don't seem to understand me. What would you recommend?

Hoarse

Dear Hoarse,

If your children are young, the only word they'll under-stand in church is "doughnut." If you whisper it, they'll sense that their doughnut and cup of juice in the parish hall following Mass are in jeopardy. You can say any-thing as long as you include "doughnut." ("I should have been a nun. I know I was never this bad in church when I was a kid. May God have mercy on your soul. Doughnut.")

Monica

Dear St. Monica,

My children have forfeited their Sunday morning dough-nuts every week for the last 10 years. Now what?

Desperate

Dear Desperate,

Use hand signals.

—One finger: Your behavior is inappropriate.

—Two fingers: I *really* mean it!

—And three fingers: The next time you enter this build-ing you'll be wheeled in feet first in a pine box. That will be *very* soon.

(You can find these signs listed in the front of most Catholic hymnals.)

Monica

Dear St. Monica,

Is Elvis up there?

A Fan

Dear Fan,

Elvis was not Catholic.

Monica

Where to Sit

You lead the way up the center aisle on Sunday, so you must decide where the family will sit. You have a choice:

1. The back half, where your children will squirm and stand on the pew and whisper, "I *can't see anything!*"

2. The front half, where the priest will give you and your noisy children a look that says, "Why aren't you sitting in the back?"

Entering the Pew

For your own safety, and the safety of that nice old couple sitting behind you laughing their heads off at your pitiful attempts to prevent World War III from breaking out, make sure the family sits child, parent, child, parent, child.

The problem is you quickly run out of parent, unless, of course, you belong to a bizarre cult that practices polygamy. In that case you're not really Catholic and you'll have to pay out-of-parish rates to send your kids to the parochial school.

A better solution is to let only three of your children sit in the pew with you and your husband. Encourage the others to sing in the choir, serve Mass, or leave home and join the convent at age six.

I Will Go unto the Altar of God

It's a great thrill for you to see your child serving Mass. You kneel straight and tall, hands folded perfectly, a solemn but dignified and respectful look on your face.

You're doing these things because your child, the altar server, is doing none of them. You're waiting for him to look at you so you can *give him a clue!*

He doesn't look your way through the whole Mass. And, of course, everyone else in the church is staring at you.

Are you having back trouble?

Performing a Ministry

Twenty-five years ago, before the Second Vatican Council, the Catholic church had no "ministries" for members of the congregation. That was for the heathen/pagan/sure-to-fry non-Catholics. But then the non-Catholics discovered and stole bingo, and Catholics said, "Oh, yeah! We'll show you!" and now there are all kinds of little jobs around the church called ministries.

Dads have the best job—they get to be ushers. Your husband has probably already left his seat to "go be an usher." The dads in most parishes have a secret agreement that one usher will whisper something to the other ushers, and then your husband and the rest of the guys will disappear toward the back of the church.

You and all the other wives are supposed to think they're preparing to take up the collection. But really they're out on the front steps enjoying a few cigarettes.

Dads have no problem taking time out from the service. But you, a Catholic mother, can demonstrate no greater act of faith than to walk up to the altar, perform a ministry, and leave your children alone in the pew.

It would be impossible for you to do this if it were not for the *universality of Catholic motherhood.*

This, as you know, means that every Catholic mother is your child's mother. And you are mother to every Catholic child.

If your kids get too far out of line, some lady a couple pews behind them will lean forward and hiss, "Just what do you think you're doing! You're in church, for heaven's sake! Knock it off! Doughnut!"

Making Religion a Part of Everyday Life

The universality of Catholic motherhood also gives you the right—the moral obligation, in fact—to reprimand any Catholic kid anytime, anywhere. For instance, if you're driving to the store and you see a boy riding his bike "no hands," you must stop your car in the middle of the street, roll down your window, and bawl him out.

How do you know if he's Catholic?

He looked guilty, didn't he?

He cringed?

He apologized?

He's Catholic.

Need more proof?

He waited until your car was around the corner before he made that obscene gesture at you.

Chapter Three

A good Catholic is a fat Catholic.

How to Cook, Cuss, and Dress Like a Catholic Mother

A good Catholic is a fat Catholic. Catholics eat everything on their plates so they can help end hunger in the Third World.

Is This a Sin?

"Finish your peas," you say to your child at the dinner table. "There are children starving in India."

17

And then you remember that vow you made when you were 11. You would *never* use the phrase your mom used so often.

Have you sinned?

Of course not. It would be a sin to allow your child to waste food. Besides, you didn't really repeat what your mother said. Her words were: "Finish your peas. There are children starving in China."

You ate those peas, so that hunger problem must be solved. As far as you know, the billions of kids living in China have all the peas they want, including the ones in that bulging envelope you sent to Chairman Mao.

A Basic Truth

You must help your children understand this basic spiritual truth: "If I hate it, it's good for me. If I like it, I have to avoid it and go to confession for even thinking about it."

This truth explains why you and all Catholic mothers have such a high regard for vegetables, especially the kind that make your child gag.

On the other hand, the road to hell is paved with candy bars.

The Catholic Cookbook

What you need is a good Catholic cookbook. This cookbook, like the one your parish put together when you were a kid, should be a collection of recipes from all the ladies in your community.

A cynic (heretic, nonbeliever, copyright lawyer) might argue that each recipe bears a striking resemblance to one printed on a box of Minute Rice or a can of Campbell's cream of mushroom soup or a package of Nestle chocolate chips.

This is not true.

Take the cookies, for example. These aren't "Original Toll House Cookies." These are "Mrs. McDonald's Cookies."

See the difference?

Keep it in mind when you submit your favorite recipe.

The First Shall Be First

"Mrs. McDonald's Cookies" are a lot like "Mrs. O'Malley's Cookies" and "Mrs. Schneider's Cookies" and "Mrs. Danza's Cookies." But only Mrs. McDonald's recipe gets printed.

Why? Mrs. McDonald submitted her recipe first.

And her sister-in-law is on the parish cookbook committee.

Remember: the first shall be first.

Everyone else will have to steal a different recipe.

A Reflection on You

The recipe you submit will tell all the other mothers in the parish what kind of mom you are.

Your recipe should be:

- Wholesome
- Tasty
- One-of-a-kind
- Complicated enough to need one exotic ingredient no other mom would have in her cupboard or would waste in some stupid recipe

"Almond-honey-glazed kiwi bourbon Tater Tots," for instance.

A Real Catholic Menu

The list of real Catholic foods is very short.

- Fish sticks
- Grilled cheese sandwiches
- Tomato soup
- Macaroni and cheese
- Tuna noodle casserole

Please note that these can be served anytime, even on Friday during Lent when eating meat is still a no-no.

To mark a special occasion, you may top the macaroni and cheese or tuna noodle casserole with smashed up potato chips.

But that's really living on the edge.

Meat

Can Catholics eat meat?

Of course.

Turkey on Christmas.

Ham on Easter.

And, the rest of the year, beans and franks.

If the family can afford it.

Final Items

That's about all you need to know about cooking like a Catholic mom. Except:

1. If you're baking angel sugar cookies and you burn the wings, just snap them off and call them choir boy cookies.

2. Plug in the parish's 55-gallon coffee pot on the parish's 84th anniversary if you want to have the coffee ready for its centennial.

3. Don't worry if your son is a cross eater. Be *very* concerned if he is a cross dresser.

"What?" you ask. "Does that mean he gets cross when he has to get dressed up?"

Very good. No. It means he likes to wear his sister's plaid uniform skirt and white blouse with the Peter Pan collar.

"What!" you exclaim.

That's right. You're doing just fine. You're supposed to act:

- shocked,
- confused, and

- naive

when any reference is made to sexual deviancy or obscene words.

Well done!

How to Cuss Like a Catholic Mother

But if you're supposed to act shocked at obscene words, how can you voice *extreme* displeasure? You can say...

(Are you paying attention? Your son is fine. Come on. It's time to move on. A lot of boys his age use hair spray. Times change.)

To return to the discussion on voicing displeasure, you may say:

- "Hell."
- "Hell's bells."
- "Oh, poop."

But only to yourself.

Out loud, you may say:

- "Lord, bless us and save us."
- "Oh, my Lord."
- "Dear God in heaven."
- "Glory be to God."
- "Holy smokes."
- "Gosh darn it to heck."

You may not say "Jesus H. Christ" but you are allowed to mutter "Judas H. Priest."

Impressing Your Children

You won't be able to impress your children with obscene words. They live with your husband, too, remember?

Instead, a Catholic mother depends on "The Lives of the Saints."

There is a grotesque story to match any situation that may arise in your home.

For instance, say you catch your son stealing cookies from that cookie jar you have carefully hidden behind a barricade of canned green beans.

Tell him about St. Doughboy, an early martyr. The Romans forced this fat and sassy Christian to eat cinnamon crescent rolls until he exploded.

Or St. Klepto, patron saint of pickpockets, who always volunteered to take up the collection at the church in Athens. One Sunday after Mass the priest accused him of stealing and he replied, "May God strike me dead if I've taken a single drachma."

And more than 2 million fell from the sky onto his head.

The miracle was that he lived. And went on to become chairman of the first parish finance committee.

Now you could spend a lifetime learning all the facts about the church's saints, but then the church might turn around and say, "Yes, well, this particular person did not really exist, but the ideal which he represents...."

And so on and so on and so on.

And your children will never let you forget it.

They may even lose their faith. (They lose everything else, don't they? And whatever the item, if it doesn't turn up at the bottom of the washing machine, it's gone forever.) Then you're responsible for them going to hell.

Modern Help

If the saints don't work, you can spend a month or two skimming a Stephen King novel. His books give you the general feeling you want to convey to your children. His stories are always filled with blood and guts and gore and pus. You can use them to frighten your children into good behavior.

For example, what happened to all the other students when Carrie went to the prom?

Lord, bless us and save us!

That's right. And why did it happen?

Those teenagers didn't intend to be home by their 11:30 p.m. curfew.

But, your children may argue (What are you raising anyway? A bunch of Jesuits?), the students missed their curfew because by that time their innards were splattered all over the high school gym.

Yes, you answer, but they had already made their decision. They had already committed a sin.

How do you know they intended to miss their curfew? your children may ask.

"*I could see it in their eyes,*" you say. "*A mother always knows these things.*"

A Catholic Demeanor

Speaking of eyes, you should always keep yours cast down, except when giving the old evil one to someone in your brood.

And you should speak softly.

Like one of the good nuns in The Sound of Music.

You should not be loud—you should be *forceful*. The only time you should yell is at a Catholic Youth Organization game. Then you may encourage your child by shouting things like, "*Rip their heads off!*"

Catholic Chic

How you dress is equally important. Once again, the ideal has been demonstrated by the nuns of old. Remember how their clothes used to cover everything but their faces? How they seemed always to be looking out from a porthole?

Shoot for that.

Get into the habit.

Ha!

Boy! Remember how much fun Catholic jokes used to be! That darned Second Vatican Council.

These days nuns dress better than you do.

Chapter Four

Chaperones are ready to throw a verbal bucket of cold water on any couple that smiles.

Dating, Love, Marriage, and Sex

Dating, love, marriage, sex.

In that order.

In that order *only*.

A Rule of Thumb

You can encourage your child to be interested in someone of the opposite sex as long as you're *sure* he or she is too young to be interested in someone of the opposite sex.

Thanks to That Good Parochial School

Your parish school helps you in this area. Teachers always have the boys and girls face off in to-the-death competition so they'll hate one another.

Students might enjoy this if the contests were whining, spitting, smashing soda pop cans with their feet, or eating chalk, but they're not. These are spelling bees and coloring contests and math quizzes and name-the-patron-saint tests. When your daughter thinks "boys," she thinks "enemy" and "pop quiz" and gets a stomachache.

No one needs to convince *you* of the value of a Catholic education.

Be sure to let your child's teacher know how much you appreciate these efforts. Tell him or her, "My daughter was so upset when she got home from school yesterday, she couldn't even eat her dinner. Thank you so much. God bless you."

Sex Education

If you don't provide some sort of sex education for your child, he or she might remain totally ignorant about this subject.

That, of course, is your goal.

Your dream.

Your fervent prayer.

But it's not likely to happen if you have a TV or neighbors living within 150 miles, or your child has a brain large enough to realize that something is going on as that young body turns into a hormone factory.

It would probably be best to honestly say, "Sex is a beautiful gift from God. It's not something dirty or cheap. It was meant to be a special act of love, a wonderful way of giving yourself completely to another person you've made a lifetime commitment to."

Yeah. Right.

The problem is that that little speech starts with the word "sex."

25

Let your husband address the subject if you have a son. He'll ignore it just like his dad did.

If you have a daughter, fall back on the helpful talk your mom gave you: "Stay away from boys."

An All-Seeing, All-Telling God

You may admit to your son that you won't always be there to see what he does. But *don't let him forget that God is always watching and God tells you everything!*

A Catholic Code of Conduct

The world, the flesh, the devil, and "Dallas" are giving your adolescent child disgusting ideas that sound *very* interesting. This is a good time to remind her: If it's fun, it's a sin.

Word Games

Unfortunately, your child will do his best to weasel out of *culpability* for his actions.

Now *there's* a good word.

Mea culpa is Latin for "my fault." There's nothing like using a word with a Latin root, and a word that has something to do with blame, to sound religious.

(*Tua culpa* means "your fault." *Tua maxima culpa* is "your most grievous fault." In the old confiteor prayer, a penitent would say, "mea culpa, mea culpa, mea maxima culpa" and strike his breast three times. If you say "tua culpa," feel free to give your child a little tap on the head. At least three times.)

Keep in mind that your child will play word games to avoid admitting he is heading for the fires of hell. Remember the story about the young lad who went to confession and was asked by the priest, "Do you entertain impure thoughts?"

He replied, "No Father. They entertain me."

The Sixth Commandment

You know that in the Catholic tradition the sixth commandment is "Thou shalt not commit adultery."

This is a favorite commandment of little kids because they have no idea what it means and no teacher or parent is about to explain it to them. As near as they can tell, it has something to do with not becoming an adult, which is just fine with them.

But then, all too soon, it is the *only* commandment they seem to worry about. You can help your child a lot if you give her a set of guidelines. A young Catholic girl needs to know what is permitted and when it's permitted. Fortunately, you have all the answers. What's a mother for?

- Smiling at a member of the opposite sex: Three months to eight years old.

- Holding hands: After two years of marriage. And in the privacy of one's own home.

- Kissing: After three years of marriage. In the dark. Eyes closed.

- Dating: After age 16. With a nice Catholic boy. But not if he has his own car. And no holding hands or kissing.

- Going steady: Never. Protestants go steady.

- You-know-what: Certainly not before marriage. And after...? Well, all right. But only to have a baby. Or two. Or 12. Or 20. Why not adopt a child instead?

- Smoking and drinking: Anytime. (You don't want your child to be mistaken for a Baptist, do you?)

- Pierced ears: As soon as she can name three saints who had them.

- A miniskirt: You say, "A *what*! Kneel down right now, young lady, and the hem of that skirt had better *touch the floor!*" (Boy, that line pops right out of the ol' memory bank, doesn't it?)

- Makeup: You say, "You have such a pretty face! Why would you want to hide it under a lot of paint that makes you look like a harlot!"

Look Like a What!?

No, you can't really say "harlot." You can say, "You look like a girl the boys would be interested in."

Or, "like a tramp."

Or, "like a girl who isn't very nice."

Or, "like a non-Catholic."

What About Your Son?

Get your son on a sports team. He has a lot of energy, and if he can focus it on football instead of sex, his Catholic high school will take first place in the division.

Just as it has for the last 25 years.

After the big game, the team can hold a car wash, then take a 25-mile hike, and then begin basketball practice. No doubt they will end up in the state tournament where team members can break a few noses and loosen a few teeth belonging to some poor unsuspecting public school kids who think athletes in Catholic schools will be nice guys.

And maybe they would be if they didn't have Father Thomas "Why-Do-You-Think-God-Gave-You-Elbows?" O'Neill for a coach.

Anyway, then there's another car wash and a hike and then track and field and a Catholic Youth Organization summer league for softball and then it's football season again and...

One, Two, Three; One, Two...

Encourage your children to take the dance lessons offered to eighth-graders in Catholic schools. They'll learn the fox-trot, the waltz, and all kinds of steps that will be absolutely useless at a high school dance.

They'll feel out of place and embarrassed at the high school gathering, spend the evening stuck to one side of the gym with their backs pressed against the folded-up bleachers, and wish they were dead.

That will help cool any thoughts of romance.

And don't forget to make your daughter wear that lovely, modest, simple dress she hates. Yeah, that ought to do it.

Why Have These Humiliating Rituals?

Why does your teen's Catholic high school even sponsor these dances? Your children have grown up watching TV programs and movies in which teen dances are lots of fun. Almost as much fun as playing kissy face in a car in the parking lot later in the evening.

Now they know how awful a real dance is.

Maybe they'll stay out of parked cars, too.

But Just In Case

Just in case a teen or two actually has fun at a Catholic dance, chaperones there—large, loud people who spent years on playground duty at the Catholic grade school—are ready to throw a verbal bucket of cold water on any couple that smiles.

They yell things like *"That's still a sin, isn't it?"*

Or, *"My husband and I have never done anything that disgusting and we've been married for 28 years!"*

Or, *"If two kids do that in public just imagine what they do in private!"*

Or, *"In some countries you'd have your hand cut off for putting it there, young man! Lucky for you we're civilized. Do that again and we're going to break your fingers!"*

The Perfect Date

Your child is going to start dating no matter what you say or do, so be sure to give her some suggestions about the type of person she should be interested in.

You might be tempted to tell her that the perfect date should be Catholic, educated, and interested in helping others. *Do not do this!*

She may think you want her to go out with the pastor.

Remember the adage: some of my best friends are priests, but I wouldn't want my daughter to marry one.

A Mixed Marriage

Your son might think you're an old stick-in-the-mud when it comes to areas of the heart, so let him know you're not opposed to a mixed marriage.

For example, you see nothing wrong with an Irish-American Catholic marrying an Italian-American Catholic.

Except that they'll have children with names like Carlo Vittorio Federigo Gallagher or Michael Sean Patrick Jacobazzi.

Living in Sin

As you well know, if a male and female non-Catholic are living together, they are "shacking up."

If it's two Catholics, they're "living together."

If it's your child and someone, they "share an apartment."

You cannot force your adult child to stop "sharing an apartment."

You *can* tell him, "I just hope you stop this sometime before I die, and lately I haven't been feeling well at all. In fact, what you're doing is killing me."

Chapter Five

No one can be baptized, married, or buried without the consent of the parish secretary.

The Life of the Parish

The astronomer Copernicus—whose uncle was a bishop, by the way—said the earth circled the sun. The church said this was heresy.

You'd have to agree.

You know the universe revolves around your parish.

A Catholic Address

As a Catholic mother, you must never give a street address when someone asks where you live. The correct answer is always, "I live in St. Such-and-Such parish."

This is a handy way of winnowing the wheat from the chaff. Say, for instance, the other person says, "Huh?" Now you know he or she is not of the one, true faith, and you can take a step back just in case this is the moment God heaves a lightning bolt at the poor, hell-bound creature.

Not that all Catholics would know where St. Such-and-Such parish is, but they—like you—know the correct way of finding out.

"Oh, is that by Our Lady of So-and-So?"

"No, it's next to Holy What's-It."

Of course.

Supreme Ruler of All

Any discussion on parish life should include the person who controls all that happens there. This isn't the pope or bishop. And it certainly isn't the pastor or some associate pastor.

Oh, no.

The person who has control is the parish secretary.

Always stay friends with the parish secretary.

Whenever you see her, say: "Honey, they just don't pay you enough."

- Or: "I looked up 'saint' in the dictionary, and it had your picture."

- Or: "You're the only person I know who's going straight to heaven!"

- Or: "I made you this fudge."

- Or: "Here's ten dollars."

Then, and only then, may you ask: "And do you know where the cord is to the big coffee pot in the parish hall?"

A Higher Authority

Always remember that no one can be baptized, married, or buried without the consent of the parish secretary.

The pastor has so many parishioners he can't be too sure who stands where, so if you visit the rectory and request something he will say "Uhhhh..." until he sees his secretary nod her head "yes" or shake it "no."

This is why you should never stop by on Saturday, her day off. Poor Father will say "Uhhhh..." until she returns on Monday.

Keys to the Kingdom

There's another reason to always be nice to parish secretaries: The secretary is the only one who knows where the extra set of keys is.

You—no matter how good you are, Mom—literally cannot get into the Catholic church without her.

Don't be offended when the secretary refuses to hand you the keys and instead walks over to the church with you.

When Jesus Christ comes to earth again in all his glory, she won't hand *him* the keys to the church. She'll say, "All right, come on, I'll let you in. And pick up that box of next Sunday's bulletins, will you? Might as well make yourself useful."

There's always something that needs to be taken from the church to the rectory or the rectory to the church, like some candles or altar clothes or a pipe organ.

To avoid carrying something, you should say: "Hello, Mary. My your hair looks attractive that way. This morning I broke my back. Could you let me into the church, please?"

The Number Two Man

Second in command at your parish is the custodian.

This is a very special vocation. You should check to see if one of your children has the aptitude and temperament for this highly regarded position.

You've probably seen the advertisement on matchbook covers: "Be a Catholic Parish Custodian." But you never sent away for the test. Here are some sample questions.

- Can you fit 8,000 keys on a single key ring?

- Do you wish the whole world smelled like pine disinfectant?

- Can you be invisible for hours on end?

- Can you get a 1906 boiler working and up to code using only coat hangers, old palm branches, and the plastic wrapping straps from this month's batch of missalettes?

- Can you flip a cigarette butt into a toilet bowl from 15 feet away?

- Can you make "damn fool kids" sound like one word?

- Can you whistle all day without using three notes in a row that sound like any tune composed since the Big Bang?

- Do you like to take complex, expensive equipment apart and say, "There's your problem. I'll get right on it after lunch."?

- Can you be on call 24 hours a day and not take a day off for 30 years?

- Does the thought of supporting your family on an income 30 percent below the poverty line appeal to you?

Leader of the Flock

You must always be nice to your pastor. He's had a hard life. He studied for years and years and years to be a firm but fair leader who would remind everyone of Bing Crosby in *The Bells of St. Mary.*

He even tried smoking a pipe just like ol' Bing, but he couldn't keep it clenched between his teeth without drooling.

Anyway, his vast, priceless preparation for the job turned out to be worth almost as much as your high school class on parenting taught by Sister Innocentia Immaculata Gattanokids.

The Death Penalty

The church opposes capital punishment, but somewhere along the line it sentenced your pastor to be *committeed* to death. The parish council. The finance council. The liturgy committee. The school board. The social action committee. The ecumenical and interfaith committee. The special committee studying the problem of the parish having too many committees. And on and on and on.

Be kind to him. When he's around, *never* say "meeting," "calendar," "agenda," or "ad hoc task force."

The New...Pastor?

Ah, you say, but we don't have one of those "old" pastors. Our parish has one of the new breed.

Well, be nice to him, too.

As you may know, the number of priests has dropped sharply over the last 20 years, while the Catholic population has been growing. At one time, a duke wouldn't get his own parish until he had been an assistant pastor for several decades.

But now...

Welcome your new pastor with open arms. He's going to be ordained pretty soon. Right after he finishes the eighth grade, four years of high school, four years of college, and four years of theology.

Invite him over to play Nintendo with one of your sons.

"Welcome, Father"

What! Have a priest-to-be visit *your* home!

Quick, paint it!

Scrub it!

Somebody find the Bible!

Lighten up, Mom. Suppose the pastor—a real priest, not a wannabe—is coming to dinner. What do you do?

Ask the rectory cook what he likes to eat?

No. Most likely he doesn't have a tiny, blue-haired octogenarian cooking for him full-time. That all changed when pizza places started guaranteeing delivery within 30 minutes. Besides, what she suggests would be what she likes to cook, not what he likes to eat.

And never the twain shall meet.

Just serve what you would normally serve. And let him get a taste of true poverty.

Danger!

If you have an older Catholic living in your home, you should warn him that the priest is coming *for dinner*. Otherwise he may harken back to the old "last rites" days and say, "I didn't know I was *that* sick," and die.

That can really disrupt a dinner party.

A New Parish Position

The school staff will be discussed in the next chapter, so that leaves only the parish Director of Religious Education.

Please notice that when you use her title you must say it with capital letters.

If you say, "Hi! Are you the new director of religious education?" she'll scowl at you. (Holy smokes! Could she be the niece of the old monsignor who ran your childhood parish?)

You must say, "Hi! Are you the new Director of Religious Education?"

Yes, she is the DRE in charge of CCD. As you know, CCD used to be the Catholic church code name for Sunday school. Catholic kids who didn't go to Catholic schools were marched to CCD class on the slim chance they might make it into heaven anyway.

Ha!

CCD stands for "Confraternity of Christian Doctrine."

You do *not* have to know this.

No one ever knew what the letters stood for except the kids who had to go to class on Saturday morning or Wednesday night, or on Sunday morning after already going to Mass. They could tell you what CCD spelled.

A Kind Word

But today you must be more concerned with the DRE, not the CCD. The head of the CCD at your childhood parish was some old nun who couldn't be allowed back into a Catholic school classroom because she'd be violating the terms of her parole. She *understood* Catholic kids who went to public schools. If you ran into her she would grab your arm and not let go until you had rattled off the Corporal Works of Mercy or the Fruits of the Holy Spirit.

Or your hand had blackened and fallen off from lack of circulation.

The new Director of Religious Education is a gentler person who has thrown away thousands of dollars getting a master's degree in church stuff, and now spends a good deal of her time begging for old magazines because the second-grade class is going to make *another* collage. She might be a little bit discouraged and it's up to you to cheer her up.

Tell her: "I bet you could make a *ton* of money selling real estate. You're still young. It's not too late."

She just wishes she could say the same to you.

The Good Mother

Never, *ever* forget that your reputation in the parish as a good Catholic mother has *nothing* to do with how you treat the secretary, the custodian, the pastor, or the Director of Religious Education.

And nobody cares how you handle your hubbie or kids.

The only thing said at the funerals of all Catholic moms who are considered successful, those who will truly be missed, is:

"She always sold an extra book of raffle tickets."

There is no higher praise.

Chapter Six

What you say in church may come back to haunt you.

Support Your Local Catholic School

Don't be surprised if you tumble out of bed early one morning, grope your way to the bathroom, glance in the mirror, and see your mother staring back at you.

Try not to scream. There's no time for panic.

This is a *school* day.

Mirror, Mirror on the Wall

Maybe you used to wonder why your mother had a copy of the "Morning Offering" prayer taped to the bathroom mirror.

It made it really hard to see anything, didn't it?

You bet it did. It made it hard for your mom to see her mom staring back at her.

But the "Morning Offering" has lost some of its popularity. Just slap up a "God loves you!" mini-poster or a "Jesus is my good buddy" bumper sticker.

It's just as hard to see around either one of those.

Up and At 'Em

There's always a lot to do before you wake the children or try to get that lump you married out of the sack. Good thing you, and all Catholic moms, wake up every morning at 1:30 with an anxiety attack.

The trick is to remember what's worrying you.

Here's a hint: it always has to do with laundry or cooking.

For example, you may suddenly remember that you promised to make four dozen raisin oatmeal cookies for your third-grader's bake sale.

Or you may recall that your sixth-grader spilled spaghetti sauce all over her uniform blouse and you forgot to toss it in the wash.

Which makes it all your fault, of course.

One of the cardinal rules of Catholic motherhood is: "It's my fault."

The Hindenburg disaster, for example.

Or Gettysburg.

Or the Crimean War. Whatever that was. It was probably started because Mrs. Crimea couldn't control her Catholic children.

A Quick Pick-Me-Up

If you find yourself having difficulty getting up that early to do laundry, try this:

Imagine how you would have felt walking into your classroom wearing a nonuniform blouse. Sister glances your way, looks down....

Boy! Does that get the old adrenaline pumping or what!

Rise and Shine

At 7:00 A.M. it's time to wake your children for school. Walk into their rooms and say, "My God, what a dump!"

This concludes morning prayers.

Packing Lunches

While your little ones are busy putting slices of cold leftover pizza in the toaster or flicking spoonfuls of grape jelly at Willard Scott, you have time to pack lunches.

Most Catholic schools don't have hot-lunch programs. Most Catholics have never tasted a corn dog.

You face a dilemma.

If you pack a nutritious lunch, your children won't eat it. If you pack trash, your kids' classmates will tell their moms, who will ostracize you for breaking the Lunch Code of the Catholic Mother (a lengthy Vatican document involving carrot sticks, bread crusts, and the annual Lenten Twinkie ban).

That's the pickle you're in.

What do you do?

Ask your oldest daughter to make the lunches. She'll pack junk food, and her siblings will love her. You can disavow any knowledge of what was in the paper sacks and play up the part about her volunteering to help her mom.

The Grass Is Always Greener

Maybe this description of a school morning sounds too ideal to you because you have the added burden of working outside your home. Don't lose sight of the advantages you enjoy:

- A whole other set of stupid people who boss you around.

- An added income that almost covers the cost of after-school day care.

- The satisfaction of feeling that you're doing a crummy job as a wife, mother, and career person.

It's Only Money

On the other hand, it's almost impossible for any family to send a child to a Catholic school unless both parents work and at least one is adept at white-collar crimes.

Your parish knows the cost may be a little steep but asks you to remember that you'll have money to spare when your child moves on to a less expensive institution like Harvard or Stanford.

Turn Trash into Cash

Catholic schools would be even more expensive if it weren't for the never-ending paper drives. Don't forget that last year the school—meaning you and all the other moms—brought in almost 438,000 tons of old newspapers. In fact, you made almost enough dough to cover the cost of the plywood shack the dads built out by the back fence to store the paper in.

The Carpool

You aren't the first Catholic mom who kissed her kids goodbye at the front door and then collapsed on the sofa.

Suddenly the house was *so quiet*.

You could hear…many children killing each other out in the driveway. Uh oh. The carpool. It's your morning.

There's an easy way to remember if it's your morning to drive several hundred screeching children to school: it's *always* your morning.

Do *Not* Stop!

Do not stop your car at the school!

Ever!

Tell the children to jump as you slowly drive by. Remind them to tuck and roll so they don't get hurt. Heave their bookbags and lunch sacks out on a second drive-by.

If you stop, even with the motor running, you'll be nabbed to help:

- Collect milk money
- Chaperone a field trip
- Shelve books in the library
- Retar the school roof

The Rumor Mill

It does no good for you to say, "I can't stay. I left the Mr. Coffee plugged in."

In fact, that could do you a great deal of harm.

Toss that simple excuse in the Catholic-school-parking-lot rumor mill and by the time you pick up the kids that afternoon:

1. You couldn't stay because you left the Mr. Coffee plugged in.

2. You couldn't stay because you left something cooking.

3. You couldn't stay because you left something cooking on the stove.

4. You couldn't stay because you had something in the oven.

5. You couldn't stay because you had a bun in the oven.

6. You couldn't stay because you're pregnant and there's a Mr. Somebody involved.

7. You couldn't stay because you're having Juan Valdez' baby.

8. You couldn't stay because you're having Juan Valdez' twins and you and Juan are planning on naming them Pedro and Inez.

Don't stop the car.

Playground Duty

You may be asked to help with "playground duty." After the children have finished their lunches, they enjoy 30 minutes of recess out on the church's blacktop parking lot, which doubles as the school playground.

Should you agree to do this?

Certainly.

If you have had at least two years experience with the United Nations peacekeeping forces in Beirut.

And you still have your helmet.

The Basic Principal

If you lack that kind of formal training, it's a good idea to stick near the principal anytime you walk out onto the playground.

Catholic school principals are still able to burn a hole in six-inch-thick steel with a single glance, and they can still intimidate hulking eighth-grade boys who are two feet taller and 200 pounds heavier than they are.

The tiny, sweet principal at your children's school can make one of those monsters sweat and shake, just like your husband does on the morning after the parish's annual all-you-can-eat-and-drink spaghetti-and-wine dinner.

Meeting the Teacher

Catholic grade school was easy when you were a girl. You said "Yester" ("Yes, Sister") and "I'm sorry" for eight years, and they handed you a diploma.

Well, the "I'm sorry" still comes in mighty handy, but you haven't "Yester-ed" for a long, long time, and your children probably never will.

The sisters have left the schools and been replaced by lay teachers.

Women.

Young women.

Younger than you.

Prettier, too.

43

Who says the church is the same yesterday, today, and forever?

It ain't so. In your day, you had to scoot over in your chair to make room for your guardian angel. This teacher has told your child to sit in the middle to "center" himself.

Your child is in love with his teacher. So is your husband. He's even asking about parent-teacher conferences.

Desperate times call for desperate measures. Mention to another mom that you heard your son's teacher left her Mr. Coffee plugged in this morning.

Chapter Seven

How to teach your child about heaven.

Explaining God to Your Children and Your Children to God

The spiritual world is a world of mystery. The church has debated unknowns from how many pin-headed theologians could sit on an angel to how Notre Dame could lose to Brigham Young University 10-7.

You may want to leave those questions to the experts, but don't be afraid to admit that there are mysteries in life. Your children will accept that. Your home, in fact, is filled with mysteries, the latest being: why did the phone bill say that someone at your house had dialed a 976 number ("HOT-BABE") 43 times last month?

Father, Son, and Spirit

You've been taught that there are three persons in one God. How is that possible?

Well, how is it possible for you, your husband, and all your kids to live in a house with one bathroom?

It's beyond explanation.

You might want to use a method perfected by St. Patrick to explain the concept of the Trinity. Pluck a sprig of clover from your backyard and tell your kids, "Just as there are three leaves on a single stem, so there are three persons in one God."

Your children will turn to each other, nod their heads in agreement, and say, "Mom has really wigged out."

He Only Has Eyes for *You!*

Always remind your children that God is watching no matter what they're doing. Then when some calamity befalls them (like they're accidentally run over by the garbage truck or they inhale a football), you can say: "God gotcha!"

Remember the story your mom told you? About the little girl who stole an apple from the ice box, sneaked out the back door to eat it, choked and turned bluer than Our Lady's veil, and died and *burned in hell for all eternity!*

That one won't work anymore.

No kid steals apples.

Make it a bag of Cool Ranch Doritos.

How Does He Do It?

Your children may ask, "How can God watch all the people all the time?"

Mothers used to have a hard time answering this. (What they said was, "Don't sass me, child.") Yours is the first generation of moms that can explain it with a good analogy.

Say: "God can see everyone at the same time the same way your father can park his rear end in the recliner with the remote control and watch six television shows at the same time."

Ah ha!

They know the truth when they hear it.

Yeah, But...

Suppose your son or daughter has been very good and something rotten happens to him or her. (Just suppose—no one said one of your kids was good.) Then what do you say?

"It's God's will."

Whoa, that sounds a little negative, doesn't it?

Better try: "I guess He hasn't forgotten about you-know-what, hmmmm?"

"In the Name of the..."

One of the first things you must teach your little one is how to make the Sign of the Cross.

This is the only way Catholics know their right from their left.

Who hasn't been in a car with a Catholic who said, "And up at the next corner take a—in the name of the Father, and of the Son, and of the Holy—left."?

On Bended Knee

Once they master that, move on to genuflecting in church. Teach your son or daughter that all Catholics genuflect toward the tabernacle when entering or leaving the pew, or crossing in the front of the church and walking by the tabernacle.

Most of them bless themselves while they genuflect to make sure they're going down on the correct knee.

A Cause for Scandal

When you were a little girl, many of the boys would bless themselves when they stood at the free-throw line in basketball or stepped up to the plate in baseball.

This custom has lost some of its popularity, which is just as well because many people found it scandalous. How could they believe in a God who let a little boy hit only 23 percent from the free-throw line or bat .117?

What Is Sin?

Because of changes in church doctrine, you cannot explain sin as easily as your mother did. She could simply say, "Sinning is doing something bad. When you sin, your soul becomes blacker than your little brother's fingernails."

Nowadays, it's easier for children to think of God as Monty Hall, host of the old "Let's Make a Deal" game show. Monty is willing to hand you $10,000 in cash, but you pick the curtain and end up with six crates of frozen broccoli.

Sinning is making the wrong choice, and wrong choices have dire consequences.

Give them an example from your own life, like whom you marry, for instance.

Life Everlasting

How do you teach your children about heaven? Use images they can understand. Heaven is

- an enormous amount of jelly doughnuts

- no siblings

- an endless supply of fresh batteries

- a school that has burned to the ground

- a different mother

- everything their little hearts truly desire

The Other Place

"What is hell?" your children may ask.

"Hell," you answer, "is what you are putting me through."

Ahhh....

Well, if that's the reason you are the way you are, they certainly want to avoid that.

Purgatory and Limbo

And then there's purgatory—a fine, old Catholic tradition that says most people aren't all bad or all good. Explain to your children that going to purgatory is a little bit like driving through a car wash before you tool into heaven.

Yes, but what about limbo? Limbo was a theory about where little unbaptized children went when they died. Limbo was "almost heaven." Going to limbo was like being sent to your bedroom: there were a lot of toys, but there wasn't any TV.

The theory has lost favor, but even if it were still popular there would be no reason to concern yourself with it.

Everyone knows where your kids are heading, right?

Two Favorite Saints

You know that Catholics believe in the "communion of saints." This means that people who were decent in life might give you a hand from the great beyond. Kind of like sending flowers over the phone.

St. Merlin Olsen, pray for us.

Your children need to understand this. They need to learn that there are patrons of particular areas of daily life. These are not "mini-gods." They're more like heavenly lobbyists.

St. Anthony is a favorite. He runs the Universal Lost and Found Department. That's been his job for centuries, although no one knows why. The origin of the tradition has been lost, and he's been so busy tracking down glasses, jackets, and hamsters, he hasn't had time to check it out.

If your child loses something and even you can't find it, you must say, "Ask St. Anthony." And your child will snort in disbelief.

"Ha!" you may answer. Lo and behold, there it is.

It may be 15 years later, but *there* it is!

If St. Tony is busy—there are a lot of children in the world, after all, and he doesn't have call-waiting—you may tell your child to take his request to a higher authority: St. Jude.

St. Jude is the patron saint of hopeless causes.

No doubt you, like most Catholic mothers, say *a lot* of prayers to St. Jude.

Holy Cards

There are many other saints, and a lot of them have their own holy cards, but your children won't care about these because they don't come in a pack with a stick of bubblegum.

No child has ever said, "I'll trade you two St. Pauls and a St. Luke for your St. Peter."

My Guardian, Dear

You also need to teach your children about guardian angels. When the Catholic Church talks about guardian angels, it's referring to spirits who love God and are sent to help children.

It's not talking about civic-minded, street-tough young people who say "yo" a lot, wear berets, and patrol the subways in major metropolitan areas.

Most likely your child wouldn't be interested in asking this second kind of angel to hover near the bed after the lights are out.

The Family That...

Many people who don't have children encourage people who do have children to pray together as a family. They believe this will bring family members closer to God.

In a way, they're right.

- Family members come much closer to meeting God face-to-face.

- Family members come much closer to killing each other.

Your children won't be interested in praying together until Nintendo comes out with "The Rosary."

Even then, they'll fight over whose turn it is.

Your kids won't be hot on before-meal grace, either. Unless, of course, Dad was the cook.

Chapter and Verse

You don't need to teach your children anything about the Bible. This is a good thing since you, like most Catholics, don't know anything about the Bible, except that the Protestants are reading the wrong version and they know a great deal about it, which makes the whole book highly suspect.

Leave it on the shelf between *Ivanhoe* and Volume I of Funk & Wagnall's *New Encyclopedia*.

If you feel the need to quote something, do what all Catholic moms do: quote Kennedy's inaugural address.

The Advent Wreath

Four weeks before Christmas, you can increase your faith by setting up an Advent wreath. The wreath is made of four candles stuck in a circle of evergreen branches. Three candles are purple and one is pink, resulting in heated arguments over which week is Pink Week.

(It's the third week. Practicing Catholics know this. Loose, fallen-away, damned Catholics don't. And the correct song is "O Come, O Come, Emmanuel," not "Happy Birthday Dear Jesus.")

Traditionally, every family member gets a turn lighting the candles before dinner begins.

As the days go by, the candles get shorter and shorter, the evergreen boughs get browner and browner, and your children become more and more nonchalant about striking matches

No one wants Christmas to come more than you do. Except maybe the fellow who sold you your fire insurance policy.

Lent

During the 40 days before Easter, the church suggests you give up something and concentrate on the everlasting.

For instance, you might give up your children and concentrate on making that arrangement last forever.

And When You Die

If explaining God to your children is difficult, imagine the tough time you're going to have explaining your children to God.

If you even get to talk to him.

What will you tell St. Peter (heaven's bouncer) as you stand before the Pearly Gates?

Tell him you firmly believe in the power of prayer. Remind him that your mother-in-law prayed and prayed all the while your husband was growing up that someday God would give him a brood of rotten children *just like him*!

Lord knows her request was granted.

Chapter Eight

Scare tactics are often necessary to keep your family on the straight and narrow.

Good, Clean, Catholic Fun

Maybe your husband and children criticize you for not knowing how to have fun.

They're wrong. All Catholic mothers know how to have fun. You just never confuse fun with having a good time or enjoying yourself.

Or smiling.

Things Eternal

It isn't easy trying to keep your husband and children on the straight and narrow path.

It isn't easy trying to get them even close enough to spit on it.

Sometimes it's tempting to let your guard down. That is why you should constantly remind the other people in your household that someday soon they'll die and rot in hell for all eternity.

And you won't be bringing them any glasses of Tang.

You'd like to, but it's not allowed.

That's why it's important for you to begin each day by reading the obituaries at the breakfast table.

Out loud.

A Good Christian Burial

The only thing better than finding an obit of someone the same age as your husband is finding one of someone you know. Then you can say to all:

"I think we should go to the funeral."

Unless the service is planned for a Saturday, your husband will say, "I gotta work," and your kids will say, "We gotta go to school."

But there's usually a rosary service in the evening before funerals.

After the Mass or rosary, be sure to say a couple of times, "You just never know, do you?"

Flash-Frozen Catholicism

Another reason you enjoy death so much is that it gives you an opportunity to make a casserole for the family of the deceased.

Be sure to use a cheap aluminum pan that you don't want returned. That dish may be in the freezer for a long, long time, what with every Catholic mother in the world bringing over a casserole, and 95 percent of them being tuna-noodle-something.

As a matter of fact, it probably doesn't surprise you to learn that the word "catholic" comes from a Greek word meaning "with noodles."

Even More Fun

You know a good death isn't the only fun in your life. There's Forty Hours Devotion and Benediction and a rousing Novena to Our Sorrowful Mother.

And what about in the car!

When a fire engine or ambulance goes barreling by, you take one hand off the wheel and bless yourself and lead the children in a "Hail Mary."

When it's a police car, right behind you, you can pray, "Ah, Christ, now what!"

Totally Bazaar

Don't forget what fun the annual parish bazaar is. It lasts only one weekend, but you get to prepare for it all year.

During the year you have to keep miles of yarn or thread with you at all times, along with needles, glue, glitter, milk bottle caps, and those plastic tabs used to close bread bags.

A couple thousand of those.

With these you can work on your Annual Parish Bazaar Arts & Craft Project during every spare moment. This year's set of four wet tea-bag holders is really looking good, by the way.

It's a shame they'll price your $857 worth of materials at 15 cents. For the set. And when your teabag holders don't sell, they'll end up on the Trinkets 'n Treasures table with the Noxzema jar votive candle and the Lord-Is-My-Shepherd quilted paperback book cover.

You could just hand the parish a check for $500 and save a lot of time and trouble, but what would the other moms say?

Darn right. Keep knitting.

On Vacation

During your summer vacation you get to travel thousands of miles and spend thousands of dollars and force your family to stop at local Catholic churches.

You can light a votive candle and comment on how much more you like the statue of Mary in your own parish church.

Don't let anyone tell you that you don't know how to have a rip-roaring good time.

The Sunday Obligation

Of course, "making a visit" while on vacation doesn't count as Sunday Mass. You should insist that your family spend all day Saturday looking for the nearest Catholic church to find out when Mass will be celebrated the next day.

You run the risk of your family becoming especially angry with you if you have the wrong schedule and they end up arriving on time for Mass.

On the other hand, they might find it interesting. They've never seen that part before.

Not since last summer's vacation anyway.

Holy Days of Obligation

Want to talk about a real treat? You know there's nothing like springing a holy day of obligation on your kids (especially the day after Halloween or New Year's Eve).

Here it is, the middle of the week, and *boom!* you hustle them all off to Mass.

Late, of course.

But that's OK. You know the pastor doesn't mind if your family comes late on a holy day of obligation. He's just so glad to see you. Some people don't even go to church on these days.

Of course, that isn't the way it used to be. It used to be that whole countries shut down for holy days. People would parade around the town square, have a big celebration, and die from the plague

Well, not everyone. The very rich would succumb to one of those naughty diseases.

This time, as you know, was called the Middle Ages. In some ways it was the best time ever. In other ways it was really the pits.

Kind of like your life, huh?

Don't lose heart. Remember what you always tell your children, and what your mom always told you:

"Things may seem bad now, but later on, looking back, you'll discover this was the best time of your sorry, miserable excuse for a life."

You Have a Dream

That's going to change someday, though. You know it. Someday the kids will be grown and out on their own and you and your husband will travel to Europe to visit Lourdes and Fátima and Knock and maybe Medjugorje—if you can figure out how to pronounce it—and any other spot where Mary stopped to say howdy.

Someday.

Retreat!

In the meantime, you can keep your sanity by spending a whole weekend a year without your family.

No fooling.

Your husband will *insist* you head off with the other parish moms for 48 hours at the local retreat house.

He'll plead with you to go, if he wakes up in the middle of the night and finds you standing over him with a rosary in one hand and a very large knife in the other.

Not some piddly paring knife.

A butcher knife.

You say, "I need some time to pray."

He'll answer, "AAAAAAAAGGGGGGHHHHHHHH!!!!!"

That means: "Sure. Fine. No problem."

You say, "Sorry. There was a thread hanging from my bathrobe. I just thought I'd cut it off. You don't mind if I'm gone for a weekend, do you?"

He won't mind. He'll volunteer to watch the kids.

You married Prince Charming.

I'll Do It

Soon he'll discover what you already know: volunteering is a lot of fun.

It's the best way to do a lot of work for no money while incompetent people yell at you.

How do you volunteer?

Well, Father asked for some people to sign up after Mass but you were busy gathering the pages from the hymnal and figuring out how to smuggle it past him to take it home and tape it together. (You aren't complaining about this, either. Ripping that book to shreds kept your four-year-old busy and quiet for a good three minutes.)

So you didn't sign up.

So the chairman called you at home.

That's right. Chair*man*.

Your husband answered the phone and said, "Just a minute. You want to talk to my wife."

So you knew it was either school or church stuff and not a radio station giving away a million dollars or an obscene phone call or something good like that.

"We need help!" the chairman whined. "Can you help?"

And you said *no*!

Loud and clear.

Absolutely *not*!

No way, baby!

Hit the road, Jack!

And this is how you said it: "Well, if you can't find anybody else, give me a call back and maybe I can help."

Boy! did you feel guilty about that!

Just imagine how the chairman felt! What it was like for him!

He had two cigarettes, yelled at his wife to bring him another cup of coffee, called you back and said, "I couldn't find anybody," and you said, "OK, I'll do it."

Whew!

You felt so *relieved*! You got to…No, wait. You *had* to…But you wanted to help, didn't you? Did you? No. You really didn't have time or energy to help out, but you felt bad about…But then you said you would and you were glad about that, but….

Are you ever confused!

After everyone else is in bed tonight, say your rosary and sharpen a knife.

It's time for another retreat.

The school board is a lifetime sentence.

You Are Not Alone

You need to spend some time with other Catholic moms, because everyone else thinks you're crazy. You are, of course, but you don't need people to remind you. And at least other moms understand why you're bananas.

The Little Ones

If it's not possible to be with Catholic moms, there are a few other ways to find support and friendship when you have preschoolers ripping apart your home 24 hours a day.

- Give the diaper bucket a name. No doubt you visit Bobby or Betty Bucket very, very often (not to mention rinsing Danny Diaper in Tina Toilet).

- Enjoy your time in Mr. Roger's neighborhood, analyzing Fred Rogers. Why doesn't Mr. Rogers go to church? Why is Mr. Rogers always talking to puppets? Why does Mr. Rogers like to change his shoes so often in public? Aren't you glad he isn't *really* your neighbor? Share your feelings with him. Yell at the TV screen. Goooooood!

- Talk to someone over two feet tall. Someone who isn't a pacifier junkie. Spend hours on the phone with aluminum storm window salespeople. With volunteers who want to pick up your old clothes and junk. With people taking surveys. ("Should the United States contribute to the United Nations?" "Is the tax system unfair to low-income citizens?" "How often do you use Cool Whip?")

- Work until you pass out and dream of talking face-to-face with someone with a little maturity. Someone who isn't always eating. Someone who isn't always fussing and whining. Someone besides your husband.

The Altar Guild

Your mom was right again! Remember? She said the best way to get over feeling sorry for yourself is to pile on more work, and before you know it, you're longing for the old days.

Sign up for the Altar Guild.

"Altar Guild" is a feudal term that means "a group of workers who clean the church but don't get paid for it while their own homes look like something even the hogs wouldn't sleep in."

As if you don't have enough to do, once a week you have to trot on down to the church and make it shine like that growing bald spot on your husband's head.

And take home some altar clothes to wash, too.

These, as you recall from your catechism classes, are the starched, ironed, white clothes used during Mass.

Starched.

Ironed.

White.

Hell.

Oh, come on! Make it a game! It's time to play, "Let's Find the Iron."

The Rite of Election

All Catholic moms feel a little lonely when they have seven or eight kids under five years old at home. But once a child reaches school age, you have many opportunities to meet with other parents.

The most notorious is the Parents' Club.

Here's a tip if your oldest child is about to enter a Catholic school: go to the first meeting of the Parents' Club. Go early. Sit up front. Raise your hand a lot.

Why?

At that first meeting, some mom—whose youngest child has just turned 40—will ask for nominations for a vacancy on the officers' roster.

Shoot that hand up!

Nominate someone.

Anyone.

Anyone but *you.*

It's a good idea to nominate someone who is not at the meeting, unless you can duck quickly when your nominee lobs a folding metal chair at the back of your head.

Up for Reelection

If you can get through the first meeting, you'll never have to worry about serving as a Parents' Club officer. Year after year, other parents will cluck about the need to have someone "with experience."

Cluck along.

Or they'll want someone whose kid just entered the school.

"New blood."

"Fresh meat."

Cluck, cluck.

If you miss the first meeting and you're nominated (and nominated means elected), you'll serve for *life*.

Having all your children grown and on their own is a cheap and flimsy excuse for submitting your resignation. Don't bother even trying. It won't be accepted.

Your only escape is death.

Even then you'll be expected to serve on committees.

Your Friends, His Friends

You may be asking if you can find support by getting together with other couples.

No.

It's not possible for a husband and wife to have mutual friends.

The Catholic moms you like the most are married to guys who sometimes, almost, sort of, just about, come close to helping out around the house.

Your husband finds this very threatening. He believes those men are troublemakers, tampering with the natural order of the universe, probably communists, undermining the system that has made this country what it is today.

Shoot, hellfire and brimstone! Some of 'em don't even watch football on TV!

Case closed.

On the other hand, his friends are all married to mousy gals who say only six words to their husbands: "Can I get you another beer?"

At the Store

One of the best places to get together with other moms is at the grocery store. Catholic mothers congregate at the day-old-bread/

dented-can aisle and the free samples of frozen pizza demonstration.

But be careful, you'll look like a complete idiot if you walk into the store without a fistful of coupons. They prove that you are a frugal shopper, a good homemaker, a wonderful mother, a loving wife, and a decent human being—not a gold-digging, money-wasting unfit mother.

You don't have to actually buy what the coupons are pushing. What would you do with a 15-ounce jar of pickled celery hearts anyway?

Besides, all mothers forget to give the checkout clerk the coupons. Except that young mom who stays so slim and has perfect fingernails.

Everybody hates her.

Take Charge! Retreat!

The previous chapter already discussed the simple but effective way to make sure you get to go on a weekend retreat. Retreats present excellent opportunities to spend time with other Catholic moms, who already know the Two Excellent Reasons for Attending a Weekend Retreat:

1. For 48 hours you don't have to take care of your children.

2. For 48 hours you don't have to take care of your husband.

"Ninety-Nine Bottles Of..."

Even getting to the retreat is a lot of fun! You can join four or five other moms in a car pool and sing your way there. They'll teach you their old favorites:

- "My Husband Is Cooking Dinner Tonight and My Children Will Have to Eat It."

- "I Didn't Do the Laundry Before I Walked Out the Door."

- "Maybe Bobby Has the Flu! (Doo-da, Doo-da)."

- "Take Me Out to the Convent."

Dinner Is Served

On Friday night you'll be served a gloppy, meatless noodle casserole.

It will taste *great!*

You didn't have to cook it.

You didn't have to serve it.

You don't have to do the dishes.

Life is *great!*

Listen!

Many newcomers get a little carried away with their praying and shout things like "*God! I don't miss my family! I can't believe how wonderful this is! Dear, sweet, Jesus, thank you!*" Don't do it. It's considered bad form.

It disturbs the silence.

Listen! Hear that? That's what no TV sounds like. Pretty weird, huh?

At your house, the only thing louder than the TV is your husband yelling at the kids to turn down the TV. But they can't hear him with the boom box blasting away.

You won't have to take a vow of silence, but you'll find it isn't necessary to talk a lot.

In fact, with just a word or two, you and the other Catholic moms can tell a whole story. These are some of the traditional tales told at the first meal:

- "Nintendo."
- "VCR."
- "Diaper."
- "Chicken pox."
- "Spam."
- "Sack lunch."

- "Oven cleaner."

- "Whine."

- "Weight Watchers."

- "Pastor."

- "Bathroom fungus."

- "Children."

- "Husband."

No, wait. That last one is a little personal. Don't tell that one until sometime Saturday.

Home Again

But then soon—very soon—it's Sunday afternoon. You're home again, and your husband and children are looking up at you with tears in their eyes.

Yes, tears.

Your family is saying, "Hey, you're standing in front of the screen." Move a little to the left. There. That's better. Listen to them sigh.

Oh, come on. They're glad you're back. In no time at all one will ask, "Are we going to eat tonight or what?"

The Luncheon

Another good time to get together with other Catholic mothers is the Annual Parish/School Spring Salad Luncheon and Fashion Show.

For this event, held in the parish hall, you wear a hat and gloves and your Nice Dress and those shoes that cost you a toe or two every time you put them on. Then you spend at least an hour and a half slinging back boilermakers and making small talk.

Things like: "Is it warm in here?"

And "I don't usually like bourbon."

And "Anybody got a cigarette that isn't one of those low-tar pieces of cardboard crap?"

Then lunch is served. On tiny, tiny plates. Very classy. Special dishes reserved for the Annual Parish/School Spring Salad Luncheon and Fashion Show.

You must not take a lot of salad. A whole radish would be too much. You have to prove to the other moms that you don't eat a lot. And neither do they. They're taking half a cucumber slice or a small black olive or one crouton. (If you want to see them eat, stop by the 7-Eleven before the luncheon and get in the chili-dog line. Get there early if you want onions.)

After lunch and a dreamy dessert *no one* is allowed to touch (make a mental note to stop by Baskin-Robbins on the way home), the fashion show begins. Stick women will walk around wearing clothes that would never look right on you, even if you could afford them.

Join the other moms looking for panty lines and laugh and hoot and point and whistle when you spot some. See if you can get that size three to burst into tears.

True friends are a gift from God.

Chapter Ten

Eve can be called an Honorary Catholic for having so much blame heaped on her.

Famous Catholic Mothers

The history of the Catholic church is cluttered with famous mothers who are admired, respected, and loved by Catholics throughout the world.

It's important that you notice the one thing almost all these moms have in common: They're dead.

Except for this one little drawback, they've got it made in the shade.

The First Woman

Technically speaking, Eve (of Adam & Eve, Inc.) was not a Catholic, but she can be called an Honorary Catholic for having so much blame heaped on her.

What was her crime?

One evening she said to her husband, "How about if we just have a fruit salad for dinner?" And all hell broke loose.

Just like at your place, huh?

She's Number One

The most famous Catholic mom is Mary. Today people tend to think her life was accompanied by a host of angels singing "Ooooo!" all the time (sounding like the Mormon Tabernacle Choir or a couple of Karen Carpenters).

Not so.

A lot of Catholic mothers are attracted to Mary because she was an unwed pregnant teenager, a widow, and a single parent who watched her only son executed.

And God really liked her.

You probably feel close to Mary because, in just about any situation, you can say a prayer to her from the heart. Something like: "Aren't kids a pain in the behind?" Or: "Sometimes life *really* stinks." And you know she understands. She's in heaven, looking down at you and replying: "Tell me something I *don't* know."

Cana, Vintage 30 A.D.

Don't forget that Jesus didn't really start cooking until Mary gave him one very large nudge.

You remember the story. Cana. A wedding party. The host ran out of wine and she said to her son, "The vino's kaput, J.C.," and he said, "Huh?"

Does that sound like a typical son or what?

So she turned to some servants and said, "Do what he tells you."

And—Matthew, Mark, Luke, and John didn't record this but you can bet the farm that it happened—under his breath Jesus said, "Ah, Ma...."

The rest, as they say, is salvation history.

What's the lesson here for you? Nag your children. It's the holy, proper, *Catholic* thing to do.

Not a Cradle Catholic

Cana is a clear example of Mary acting in a Catholic way, although she was a convert.

Don't dwell on this point.

Yes, she was Jewish, but if you ask any Catholic mother about Mary, you will hear that she was Irish, Italian, French, Mexican, Filipino, Korean, Bolivian, American, Republican, a Laker fan, an Amway distributor, etc., etc., etc.

Just like Santa Claus.

And God.

God the Mother

Speaking of the Big G (little O, little D), one time a pope said that in many ways God is more like a mother than a father.

Meaning God sets a darned nice table and doesn't turn the air blue when he tries, unsuccessfully, to start the lawn mower.

Holy Mama

Traditionally, the church has been called Holy Mother. This is because she watches over her members, who ignore her almost completely except when it's convenient or they want something.

That's a mother-child relationship, all right.

The Exceptions

There are two famous living Catholic mothers. One is Mother Teresa of Calcutta. You and the other moms think she's swell because she says that nothing is more important than love and that doing menial, thankless, dirty jobs is a good way to show that love.

That sums up your existence.

It surprises you that your husband and other men say they like her, too.

They like her because she always wears the same outfit whether she's accepting the Nobel Prize or going to the corner market for a loaf of bread.

"And Now, Heeeeeeeere's..."

The other famous living Catholic mother is Mother Angelica. Perhaps you've seen her on cable TV. She's a proud graduate of the Barbara Bush School of No-Frills, No-Nonsense, No Guff from Guys.

While leaders in the American Catholic church were wailing and gnashing their teeth and saying, "Shoot, we gotta get some kind of show on the old tube to offset those fundamental evangelists!" she started her own network.

Nobody told her she couldn't do that without a pot of money, a lot of three-piece-suit types offering advice based on market-research studies, and a large committee that meets four times a year at a very swank hotel.

Don't blame her. She just didn't know any better.

It seems she thought that if something needs to be done, you just go ahead and do it.

Oh, sure, let the menfolk go on jawing, but they better just *stay out of the way!*

An Oldie but a Goodie

The first American saint was Mother Frances Xavier Cabrini. She was born in Italy and later became a U.S. citizen. She wanted to be a missionary in China, but the closest she got was the West Coast of the United States, and since she wasn't a surf bunny she didn't consider this a really big treat.

She's a good example for Catholic moms because she never got what she really wanted, just like you've never seen the bottom of the laundry hamper no matter how many loads you do in a single day.

She started hospitals and orphanages and all sorts of good stuff all over the United States and South America, and many moms say a prayer or two to her for very special help.

A good example is when you have a car full of screaming children and you can't find a place to park. You say: "Mother Cabrini, park my machinery."

Boom! An empty space.

Maybe even one with time on the meter.

But like St. Anthony—those Italians are really something, eh?— Mother Cabrini doesn't have call-waiting. If the line is busy, try Mary.

Say: "Hail Mary, full of grace, help me find a parking space."

It's a Miracle

Sure, cynics will scoff at the idea that the Mother of God or St. F.X. Cabrini will provide you with a slot for your Malibu wagon, but what do they know?

It works.

Most people have a really screwed up idea of what a miracle is. Who cares if the paint blister on the side of the garage looks like Jesus, or an apple fritter down at Winchell's bears a startling resemblance to Da Vinci's "Last Supper"?

Think about the miracles Jesus performed (after Mary's nudge). He took care of people. He never said, "Check it out. Here's a rutabaga that looks just like Moses."

No way. He said, "Am I the only one who's hungry, or could everybody go for some fish and chips?"

Patron Saint of Power Forwards

Mother Cabrini was the first American saint, but Mother Elizabeth Ann Seton was the first American-*born* saint.

She's had a bit of a PR blitz since Seton Hall came so close to winning the Final Four college basketball tournament. Seton Hall students were the ones who said, "All right, it's party time, dudes! Let's go back to the hotel and have a Mass!"

Talk about your inexplicable, supernatural occurrences.

Mother Seton started the parochial school system in America back in 1813. It took the Vatican decades to crush the ugly, vicious rumor that she scooped up a ton of stock in corduroy pants, plaid skirts, and soap-and-water saddle shoes before she launched her little venture.

A Saint's Life

Maybe it doesn't help you to think about this wonderful nun who was such a terrific person when your life is a black hole. Consider this: Mother Seton was a rich Episcopalian who married well and lived on Wall Street. Then the money went bye-bye, her husband died, and she was a young, broke widow with five children.

She started a boarding house for school boys.

That is a very good definition of "desperation."

She was 30 when she and the kids became Catholics. Then she started a religious order of nuns. Some of her kids were nice and some were real stinkers, and in general her life was one heck of a lot of work. She died of TB when she was 46.

Does that sound like someone who could understand what you face every day?

In fact, considering what you went through this morning alone, it could be you're well on your way to sainthood.

The Bilingual Saint

Maybe the idea of your being canonized is too hard to imagine. But then St. Elizabeth Ann probably never thought some 6-foot-11-inch forward with "Seton" written across the front of his undershirt would be saying, "We just couldn't connect with the three-pointers, and they were really executing the zone defense and killing us on the fast break."

Huh?

She was fluent in English and French. She didn't speak basketball.

When in Rome

Most likely the church will never officially recognize all the trials and tribulations you have endured. Perhaps that's just as well. It means your descendants will never have to zip over to Rome and sit through a very, very long ceremony and whine:

- "How come I gotta wear a tie? I can't *breathe!*"

- "I can't see anything!"

- "These new shoes gave me a blister!"

- "Is it over?"

- "The cab driver said it's near the Spanish Steps, but this map doesn't show any McDonald's!"

Chapter Eleven

Grandmas can experience the joy of motherhood vicariously.

How to Be a Catholic Grandmother

It's not easy being a Catholic grandmother. You have to be very, very careful.

Say your grown-up son tells you, "I don't know what I'm going to do with Timmy. He just won't behave in Mass."

Your natural reaction would be to fall on the floor and roll around laughing until you got a severe side ache.

Do not do this!

You could break a hip.

It's much safer to *sit down* on the floor and then begin rolling and laughing.

When Is Enough?

You don't want to be rude, of course. So how long is a grand-mother allowed to laugh hysterically at the plight of her child?

Generally speaking, if you're still able to squeak out "There *is* a God!" then you can keep going for a little while longer.

Your child won't be laughing, but your grandchild will think you're a lot of fun.

Not at all like Mommy and Daddy described you.

Children vs. Grandchildren

No doubt you've noticed that you feel differently about your grandchild than you felt about your own son or daughter.

Maybe you've had a hard time putting those feelings into words.

Try these: "I like my grandchild."

Why is this? It's because you're not responsible for teaching this little one right from wrong or the Ten Commandments or why good little Catholics don't spit on the sidewalk or hot-wire cars.

All you have to do is give hugs and pass out graham crackers and tic tacs.

Even when your grandchild is very, very small, you have the right to hold him and say: "What a beautiful baby. I'm the happiest woman in the world. Uh oh. Smells like someone made a boom-boom. Go see Mama."

Don't forget to say a silent thank-you prayer. And give your child a big smile as you hand the baby back and think about all the boom-boom she handed you all those years.

It's a Miracle

God uses the birth of a grandchild to change horror stories into funny stories.

For example, you always thought that "The May Day Karen Was Supposed to Crown the Statue of Our Lady but Drank Four Pepsi-Colas and Got Very Nervous and Threw Up All Over Father O'Connell" was a horror story.

But then you begin telling it to your granddaughter. Your daughter starts to squirm and sweat and your granddaughter starts to laugh, and you realize this is really a funny, funny story.

You never noticed that before!

Wisdom *does* come with age.

Grandma's Fables

You have hit the Catholic mother lode.

Your child can't remember anything that happened to him before kindergarten, so you can make up anything you want, as long as you begin the story with "You were about four when..."

Helping Your Child Feel Old

It seems like only yesterday that your son or daughter was out raising Cain, figuring he or she would live forever.

That might have been 15 or 20 years ago.

Mention it.

"It's been 20 years since..."

Twenty years! "No, Mom," your child will say. "That can't be right."

"My mistake," you answer. "It's been 22 years since...."

You owe it to your grandchild to finish the story.

"...since your daddy got picked up for mooning Sister Scholastica and the police brought him home and...."

What's in It for You?

Remember all those years when "going on vacation" meant cramming eight kids in the Rambler and driving to some cruddy state park and living in a tent and cooking meals over a sputtering campfire and sleeping on the ground and... and... and....

Pack your bags, Grandma!

You can go anywhere you want, all expenses paid, if you begin your stories with: "I saw an ad for a Caribbean cruise. It reminded me of the time streaking was the fad and you...."

Or "I've always wanted to see the shrines at Lourdes and Fátima. I can't help but think of them when I remember the time you went to that party and Bobby Folsom's older brother bought all that beer for you kids and you...."

Your child will have you on a jet faster than you can say, "Visa Gold."

Give a Little

But being a Catholic grandmother isn't all taking and no giving.

For instance, if your granddaughter is 12 or 13, give her a tight leather miniskirt that comes up to *here* and a flashy halter top that goes down to *there*.

"Mother!" your daughter will explode. "Have you lost your mind!"

Apologize.

"I'm sorry," you can say. "I thought maybe these still had some wear in them. I found them last week when I was cleaning out the closet in your old bedroom."

And for You, My Child...

Cleaning out the old homestead is a wonderful pastime. For years and years your children gave you gaudy pieces of junk for Christmas, Mother's Day, and your birthday and you saved it all.

Now you can give it back to them. With a little note: "I just couldn't throw these things away because they mean so much to me. I know they will mean the same to you. I want you to have them. Before I die."

Be sure to add those last three words.

That final twist of guilt is what makes this a truly Catholic moment.

And for Your Grandson

Speaking of cleaning out stuff, it's a good time to empty that one drawer crammed with bits of old rosaries and broken statues and palm branches dating back to the Pius XII Administration. You know you can't throw it away because it just might be blessed.

Wait until your grandchild is visiting and then say, "And this is Grandma's special drawer. Filled with *treasures*." Nothing personal here, but the kid is a real chump. (Just like yours.) He'll take it all.

It's important that you remind him: "And don't show Daddy what Grandma gave you until you get home."

Added Insurance

Maybe Daddy will bring it back the next time they visit and say, "Here, Mom. Thanks, but Johnny isn't old enough for this yet. He just doesn't appreciate it."

Nice try, kid.

You say: "Then hang on to it for him, will you?"

And: "See this half decade of a rosary? This was your great-great-aunt's. She wanted you to have it but I just couldn't part with it until now. She would want Johnny to have it. I want Johnny to have it."

"Before I die."

Game, set, and match.

Religious Art

Just about the time you get your house cleaned out, finally convincing the kids it's not a free mini-storage warehouse, it becomes an art gallery.

Your child will bring over thousands of lousy crayon pictures your poor grandchild was forced to draw "for Grandma." These, of course, replace all birthday, Christmas, and Mother's Day gifts. (Your child brings reams of them when he comes by to borrow money.)

Your kid might be afraid you can't see the artistic talent these drawings reveal. This is when you say: "The child is a *genius*! This is a picture of the first Christmas, isn't it?"

Or "the Annunciation."

Or "the Last Supper" (if it happens to look like an apple fritter).

Or... but you get the idea.

Say it's something religious and your child will have to agree for fear you won't hang it on your refrigerator.

"And It's Only..."

When the grandchildren get a little older they'll pester you to buy junk to support the parish school. Things like the Greatest Chocolate Bar in the Whole Wide World and Two Neighboring Planets. Eight dollars for a half-ounce bar.

Buy a lot. Then give it all back to your grandchildren on the sly. Tell them, "And say a little prayer for Grandma, OK?"

This is not really a bribe. It just has all the appearances of a bribe.

The Death of Liberalism

There is no greater joy than watching your own grown child—that hellion—embrace dogma and discipline.

This is a classic example of the correct use of the phrase, "scared the hell out of." As in: "Becoming a parent scared the hell out of my son."

Now that your child is so tight, you can loosen up. You can say to your school-age grandchild—while his daddy is listening—"Doesn't it seem unfair that you have to go to Mass *every* Sunday?"

And your son will say, "What Grandma means is...." And he'll be off on some lengthy explanation that no one will listen to.

You just can't believe what a kosher Catholic he's become. Watch his jaw hit the floor when you say: "You know, when we get to heaven we may see Mary wearing brown and St. Joseph wearing blue."

Heresy! Mary *has* to be in blue.

Tell him you bought the latest Shirley MacLaine book.

And from now on you want to be addressed by your fourth-century-B.C. name, "Boola-Boola."

What Is Truth?

You have to remember that your grown child is confused. Who can blame him?

You were the one who told him he could grow potatoes in his ears, there was so much dirt in there, and when he made a face like that, God was going to freeze it that way, about the same time you told him religion was important.

Yeah. Right, Mom.

But now, somehow, he's beginning to get the idea that it is. This being alive business creates a lot of questions and not a lot of answers. And his own kids are starting to ask some good questions already.

Give him a break.

Take him in your arms, hold him close, and tell him, "Every parent wants the best for his or her kids. All you need to remember is..." and then mumble something.

"What?" he'll ask.

"I said 'Go scrub those ears!'"

"Mom!"

Grandma Knows Best, But No One Ever Listens!
by Mary McBride

Mary McBride instructs grandmas who have been stuck with babysitting how to "scheme, lie, cheat, and threaten so you'll be thought of as a sweet, darling grandma."

Order #4009

Don't Call Mommy at Work Today Unless the Sitter Runs Away
by Mary McBride with Veronica McBride

In this guide for working mothers, Mary McBride gives moms hints about everything from choosing a babysitter to choosing a business suit. "More valuable to the working mother than a cart full of frozen dinners." —Phyllis Diller.

Order #4039

Mother Murphy's Law
by Bruce Lansky

The wit of Bombeck and the wisdom of Murphy are combined in this collection of 325 laws that detail the perils and pitfalls of parenthood. Cartoon illustrations by Christine Tripp.

Order #1149

Dads Say the Dumbest Things
(Available April 1990)

by Bruce Lansky and Ken Jones

Here's a hilarious book that has every funny (and stupid) expression fathers use to educate and discipline their children...and drive them up the wall. It also includes 19 photos of TV's favorite fathers, plus humorous quotes from their TV shows.

Order #4220

The Parents' Guide to Dirty Tricks
by Bill Dodds

Since kids think nothing of lying and cheating to get their way, here's an outrageous book that shows adults how to fight fire with fire. It teaches parents how to get kids to eat green vegetables without a whimper, how to lose your kids on a nature hike, and more.

Order #4190

The Dictionary According to Mommy
by Joyce Armor

Here's a dictionary for mothers that's a lot closer in style to Bombeck than Webster. It contains 500 all–too–true definitions that every mother can relate to and every mother–to–be had better study.

Order #4110

Order Form

Qty	Title	Author	Order No.	Unit Cost	Total
	Dads Say the Dumbest Things	Lansky/Jones	4220	$5.95	
	David, We're Pregnant	Johnston, L.	1049	$5.95	
	Dictionary According to Mommy	Armor, J.	4110	$4.95	
	Don't Call Mommy	McBride, M.	4039	$4.95	
	Do They Ever Grow Up?	Johnston, L.	1089	$5.95	
	Eat a Pet Cookbook	Jones, R.	4180	$6.95	
	Empty Nest Symphony	McBride, M.	4080	$4.95	
	Grandma Knows Best	McBride, M.	4009	$4.95	
	Hi Mom, Hi Dad!	Johnston, L.	1139	$5.95	
	How to be a Catholic Mother	Dodds, B.	4230	$4.95	
	How to Survive High School	Lansky/Dorfman	4050	$5.95	
	Italian Without Words	Cangelosi/Carpini	5100	$4.95	
	L.I.A.R.	Thornton, R.	4070	$4.95	
	Modern Girl's Guide to Everything	Cooke, K.	4090	$4.95	
	Mother Murphy's Law	Lansky, B.	1149	$3.95	
	Mother Murphy's 2nd Law	Lansky, B.	4010	$4.95	
	Over the Hill Survival Guide	Feigel/Walker	4210	$5.95	
	Papal Bull	Sullivan, D.	4060	$4.95	
	Parents' Guide to Dirty Tricks	Dodds, B.	4190	$4.95	
	Playing Fast & Loose With Time & Space	Mueller, P.	4100	$4.95	
	Strange But True Facts About Sex	Smith/Gordon	4240	$6.95	
	Weird Wonders, Bizarre Blunders	Schreiber, B.	4120	$4.95	

	Subtotal	
	Shipping and Handling (see below)	
Meadowbrook Press	MN residents add 6% sales tax	
	Total	

YES, please send me the books indicated above. Add $1.25 shipping and handling for the first book and $.50 for each additional book. Add $2.00 to total for books shipped to Canada. Overseas postage will be billed. Allow up to 4 weeks for delivery. Send check or money order payable to Meadowbrook Press. No cash or C.O.D.'s please. Quantity discounts available upon request. Prices are subject to change without notice.

Send book(s) to:

Name_____

Address_____

City_____ State_____ Zip_____

☐ Check enclosed for $_____, payable to Meadowbrook Press
☐ Charge to my credit card (for purchases of $10.00 or more only)
☐ Phone Orders call: (800) 338-2232 (for purchases of $10.00 or more only)

Account #_____ ☐ Visa ☐ MasterCard

Signature_____ Exp. date_____

Meadowbrook Press, 18318 Minnetonka Boulevard, Deephaven, MN 55391 (612) 473-5400

Toll free (800) 338-2232